WHISPERING TONGUE
PUBLISHING

XYLOBHONE
A Boner-fied
Alphabet Book
For Men only!
Created by Harold Cummings

The Human Penis

The penis is a fascinating friend. With just for the purpose of eliminating urine, it is enough to preoccupy oneself. It is like a pen. You can draw in the sand, the snow or on the pavement with its amber ink. You can reach far with its pressurized golden shower and you can glaze over rocks and wet your toes or others. Early in life you learn you have a most convenient tool long before you learn the multipurpose of this tool. Your relationship with your penis grows stronger with time. As you grow, it grows. The erect penis increases the lure and mystery as well as the bond. The erect mature penis with its ejaculating attributes increases one's relationship with it at the speed of light. Thus, due to the power, the persistence, and eventually the need to hunt fulfilling nature's mission to propagate or to please may overcome you.

Naming and Naming Yours

Naming things has been a human practice since the human race began. We humans name everything, and rightfully so. Communication is essential to our survival. Naming takes many forms and has many functions. The naming of male genitalia has been an extensive pursuit over time and across cultures. It is a practice that continues in groups, with couples, and individuals.

Young men are introduced to various names of their genitalia at a young age. These names are remembered and shared. As young men grow, the list of penis names expand. These names promote a bond based around the fact that all males have an external and often demanding pleasure center.

Throughout your life, you will be exposed to many creative synonymatic names for the human penis. You, your friends and your partners will also contribute to the rising list. These names can be categorized. In this book, "_Xylobhone, An Alphabet Book for Men Only_", new names will pop-up accompanied by simple yet clever illustrations. Enjoy your journey through this alphabet book. Take the _Xylobhone_ ride around the world from A to Z into what I call "Dick Literacy".

Harold Cummings

Arrow
Ankle Spanker
Appendage
Anaconda
Anal Impaler

Beef Whistle

Boa

Best Friend

Blaster Master

Bacon

Big Boy

Bazooka

Bud

Bearded Dragon

Baby Maker

Banana

Birdie

Baloney Pony

Boat

Boy Toy

Beast

Belvedere

Blow Stick

Bottom Baster

Bat

Broomstick

Boner

Bed Snake

Baby Arm

Bellend

Captain Cucumber

DRIPULA

DING-DONG	DIPSTER
DONKEY DONG	DICK
DRILLINGER	DONG
DIPSTICK	DOODLE
DUDE	PISTON
DING-A-LING	DARTH - MATER
DOG BONE	DINGY
DONG	DIRTY DOG
DOC	DRUMSTICK
DRILL	
DIGGER	

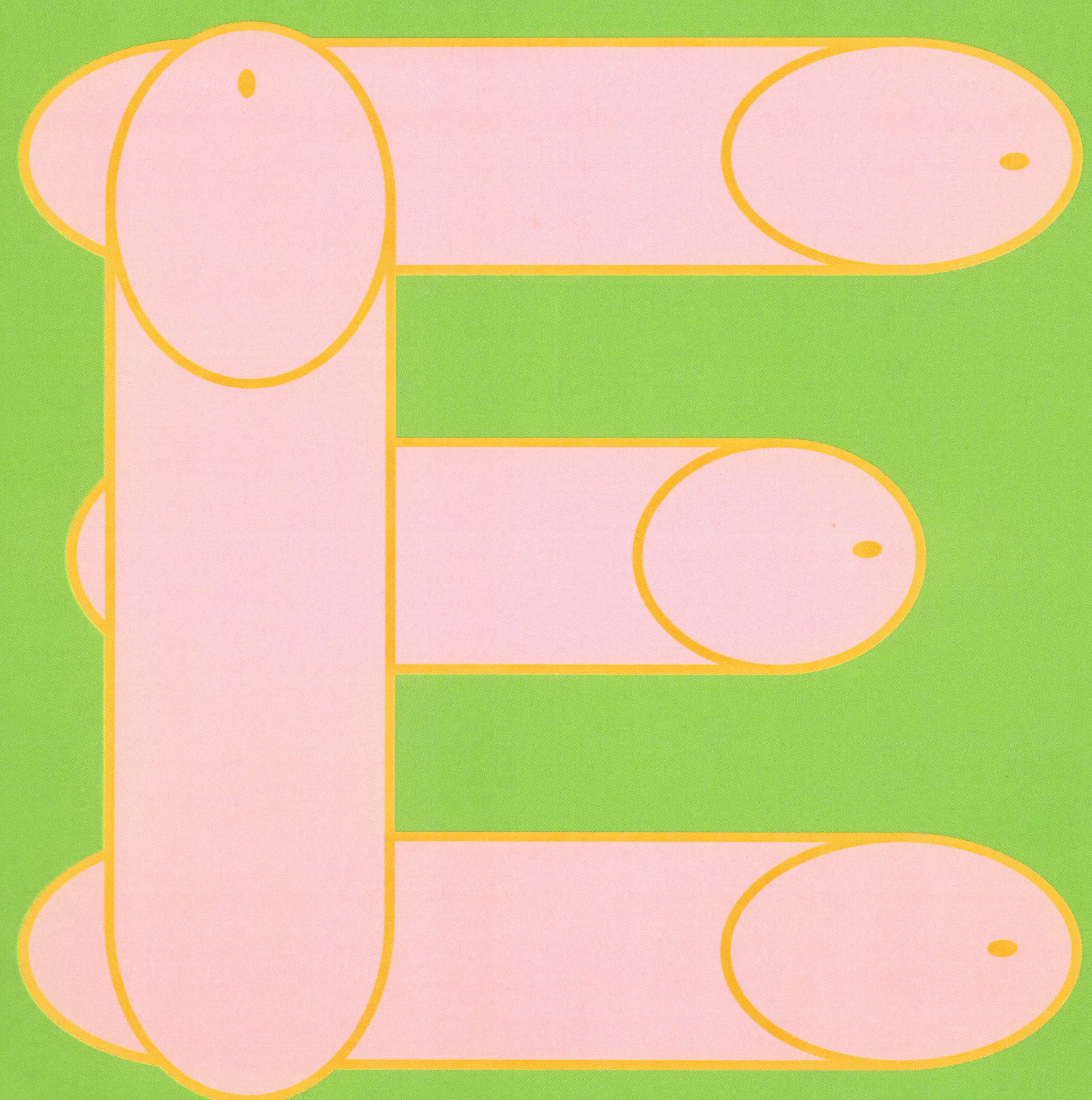

Elvis
E.T.
Erection
Erecto
Erecto-magnificent
Eruptoe
Mt. Etna
Mt. Erebus
Elvis

Firehose

Frank
Finger
Funny Man
Fuck Ferret
Flesh Flute
Filler Thriller

Fabulous Freddie
Faithful Friend
Frequent Flyer
Flesh Fruit
Footlong

Girtha
Giraffe
Golden Rod
Groin Ferret
Gherkin
Girth
Gold Finger
Gravy Master

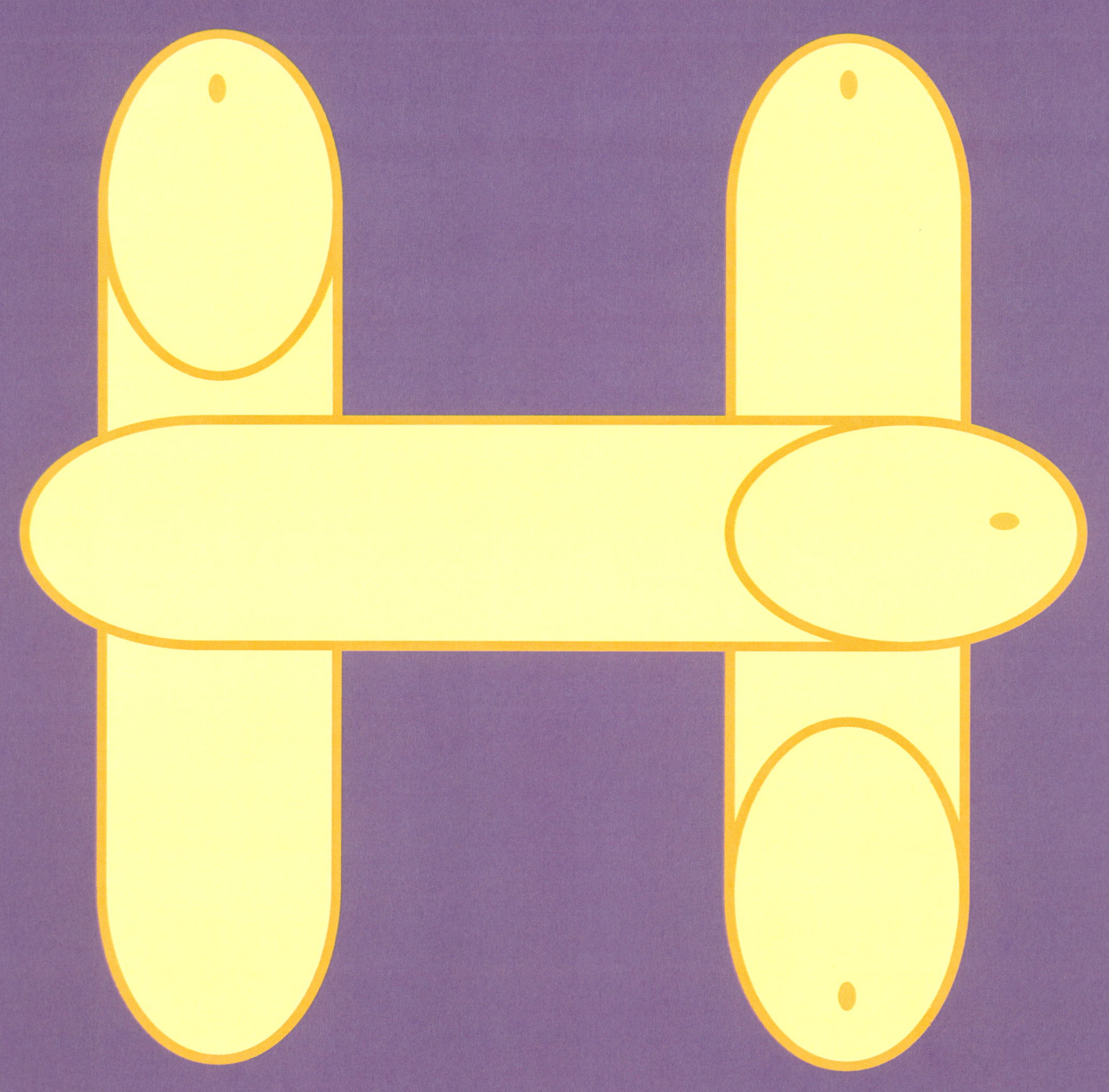

Hatter

Helmeteer, **Helmet Head**, *Hairy Canary*,
Horn, Happy, *Hard On*, Hog, **Hardy**, *Hairy*,
Hot Rod, *Ham Bone*

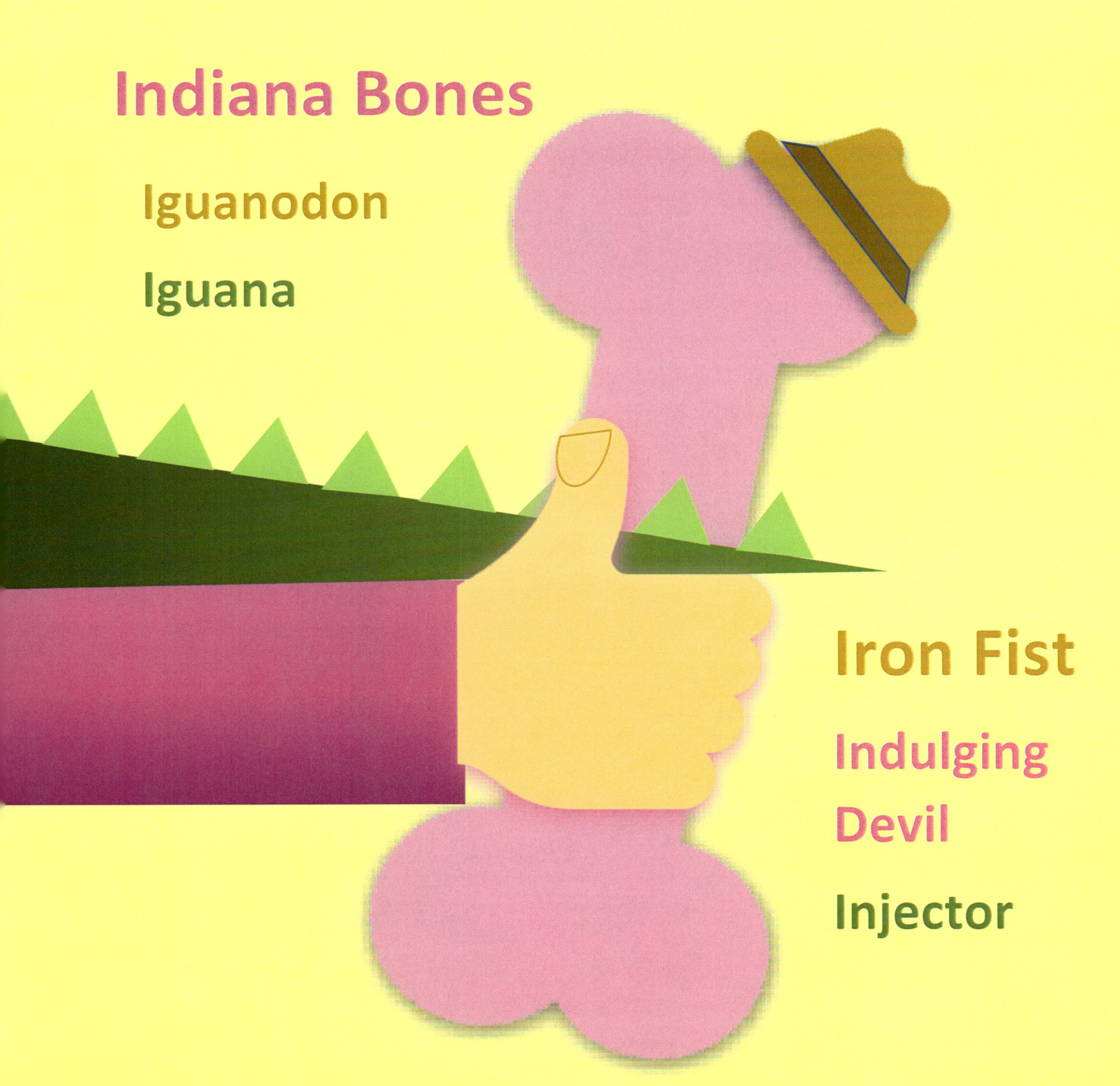
Indiana Bones
Iguanodon
Iguana
Iron Fist
Indulging
Devil
Injector

JACK the DRIPPER
Jack the Dipper
Just-in-beaver
Junior
Jock
Johnson
Jolly Stick
Joystick
Juicer
Junk

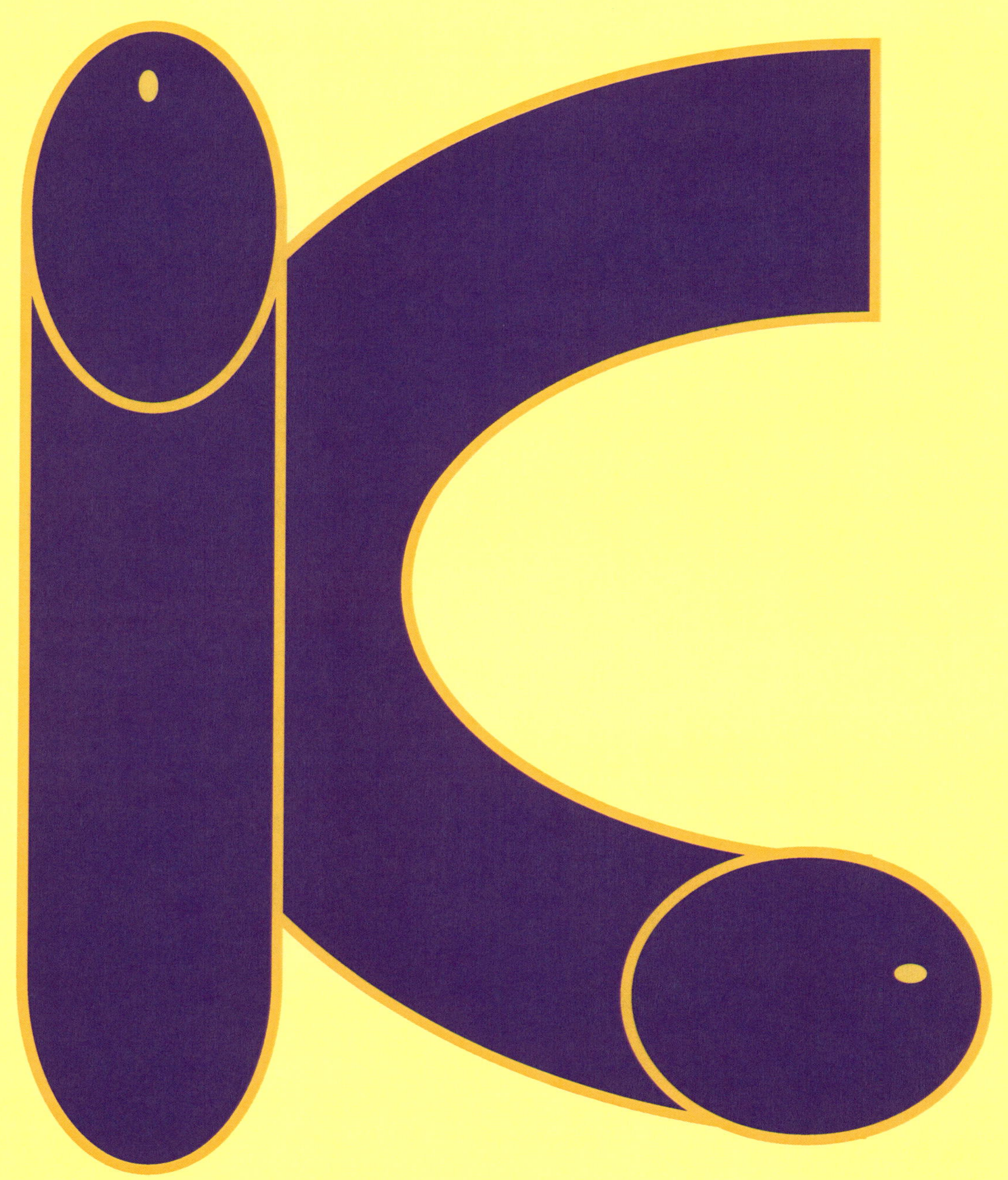

King of the Jungle
Killer
Kolbasi
King
Kielbasa
Knob
Knob Goblin
Knight
Krull the Warrior King

Dearest Love Plunger,
Little Man, Lap Lizard,
Long John Silver,
Longfellow, Little Finger,
Love Muscle, Lava Leon,
Lead, Love Stick,
Lead Pencil...

Love,

Lipstick

Meat Popsicle

Magic Wand

Main Vein

Master Blaster

Manhood

Mr. Cum-lately

Mushroom

Matador

Member

Middle Leg

Monster

Mr. Sniffles

Meat Stick

Meat Whistle

Meat Thermometer

Meat

Mini-me

Nutcracker

Naughty Norman

Nubby Nick

Nutty Buddy

Nature's Scythe

Nightstick

Nightrider

Navigator

Nozzle

Nipper

One-Eyed Snake

Old Faithful

One-Eyed Pete

Old Fella

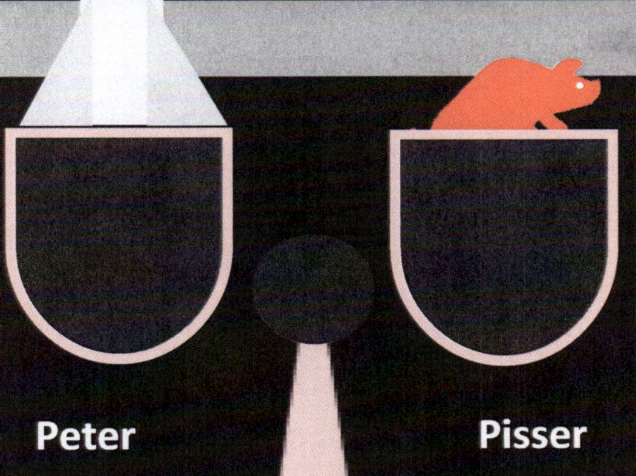

Pocket Rocket
Penrod
Pubic Pony
Pink Torpedo
Pork Injector
Pork Sword
Phallus
Percy Pecker
Pee Wee

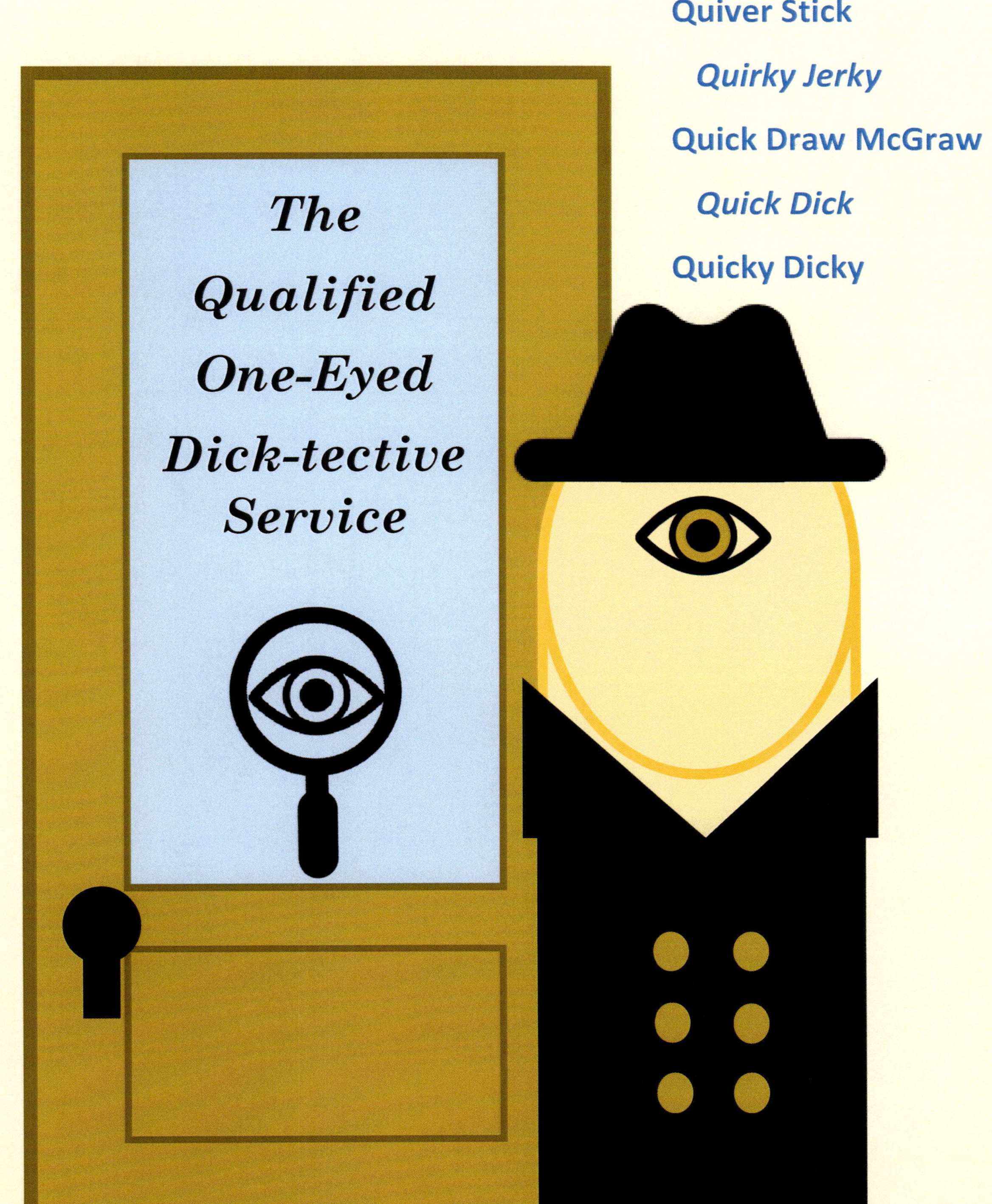
The
Qualified
One-Eyed
Dick-tective
Service

Quiver Stick
Quirky Jerky
Quick Draw McGraw
Quick Dick
Quicky Dicky

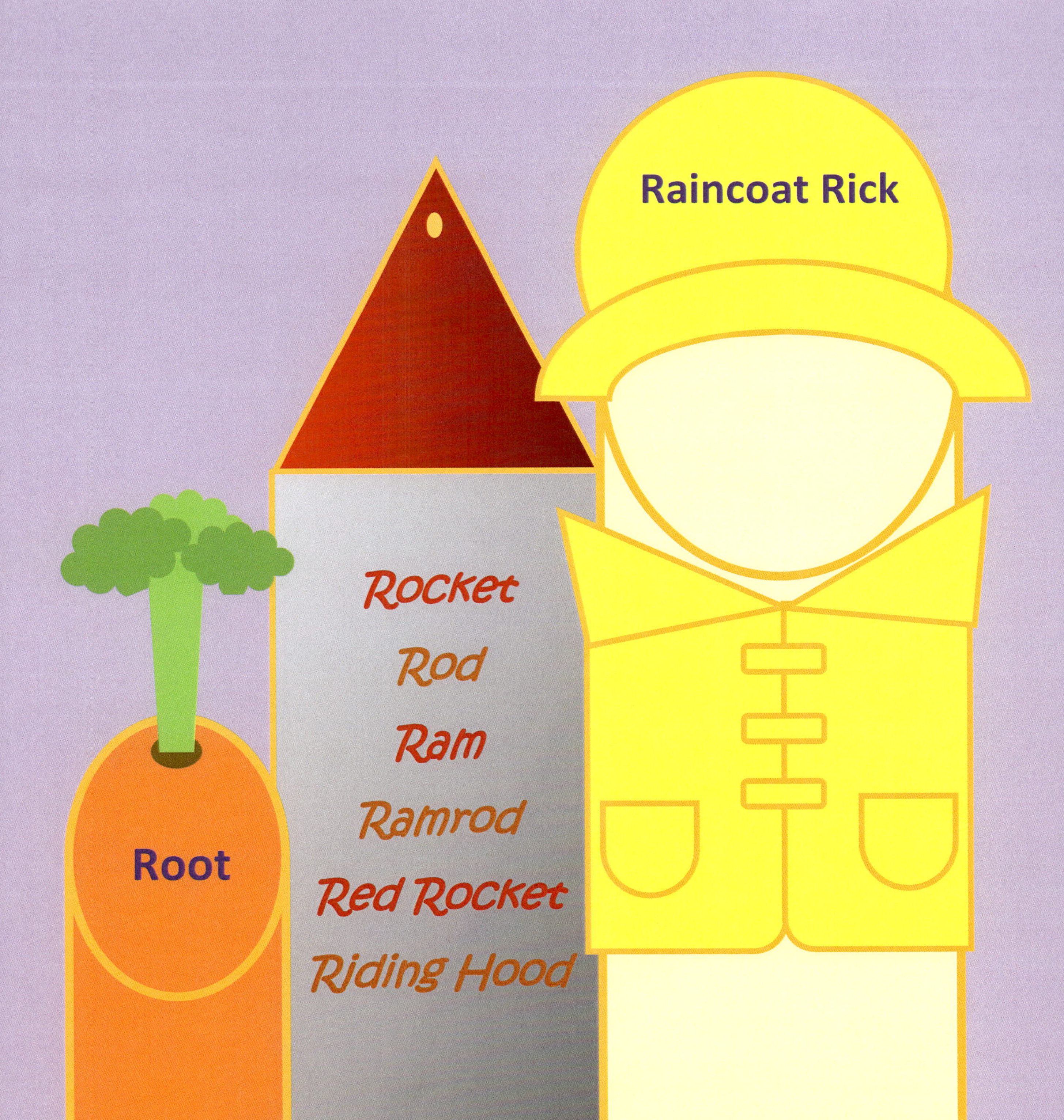
Root
Rocket
Rod
Ram
Ramrod
Red Rocket
Riding Hood
Raincoat Rick

Schlong
Spear
Shank
Snasage
Studley
Skin Flute   Speminator
Straight Eight   Slippery Servant
Silkwood   Seed Smacker

Sock Puppet

Slipappopotamus

Stem
Stretch
Shaft
Skiff
Slider
Studley
Sausage
Salami

THOMAS
THOR'S HAMMER
THIRD LEG
THING
THINGY
TUNA CAN
THE BIG DIPPER
TOOL
TRUNK
THE BUS
Trouser Trout
Trouser Train
Turtleneck
Tubby
Tube
Turkey
Turtle
Trouser Monkey
Tin Soldier
Trouser Snake
Taco Warmer
Tally Wacker
Tunnel Plunger
Thickster
Trickster

UNICORN

Unsung Hero
Uterus Unicorn
Ulysses the Uncut
Unbelievable Weevil
Unit
Undercover Dicktective

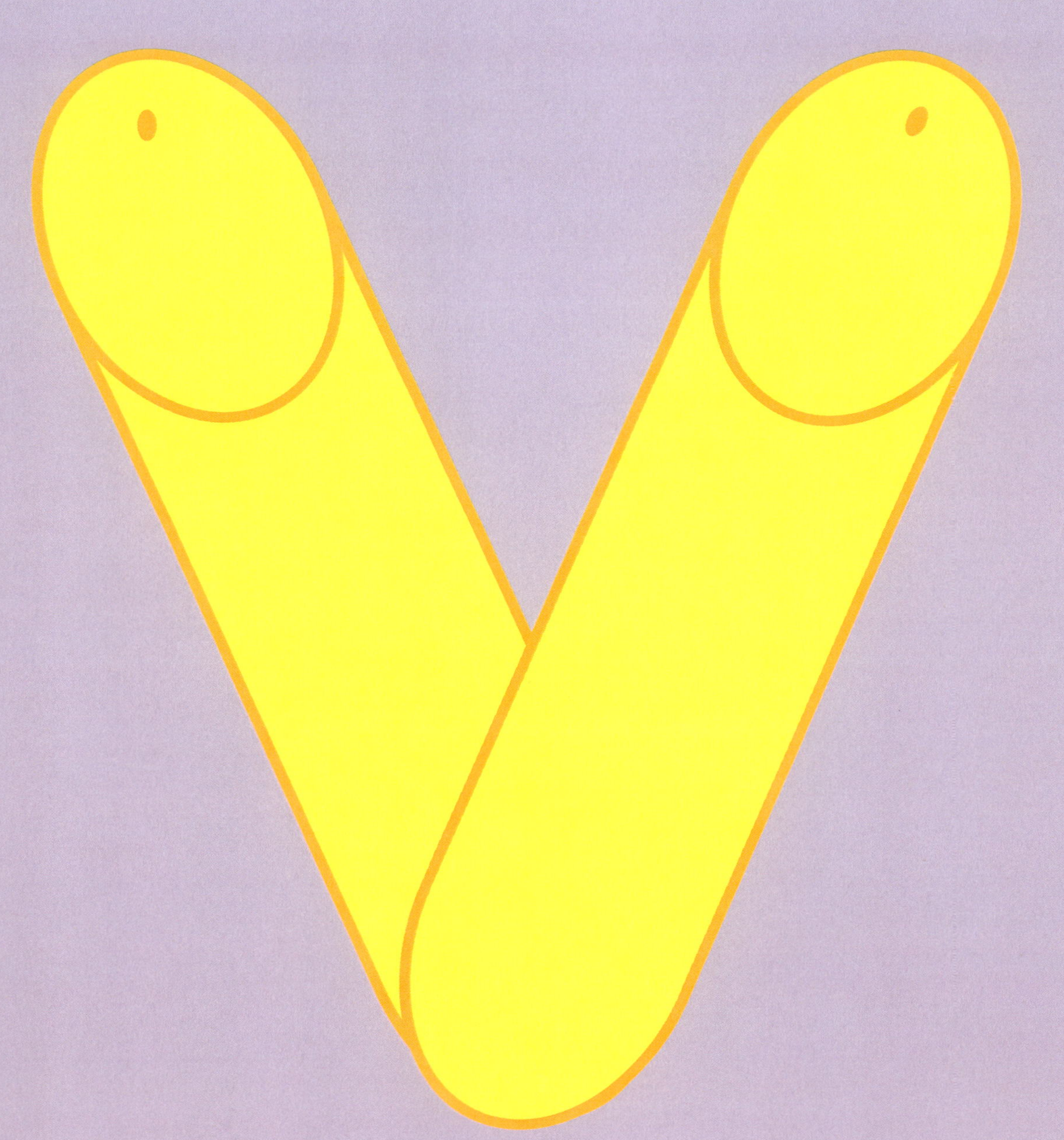

VOYAGER

Vessel
Vivacious Victor
Vehemente
Volcanic Nick
Varmint
Velvet Varmint
Vigor Trigger
Vein

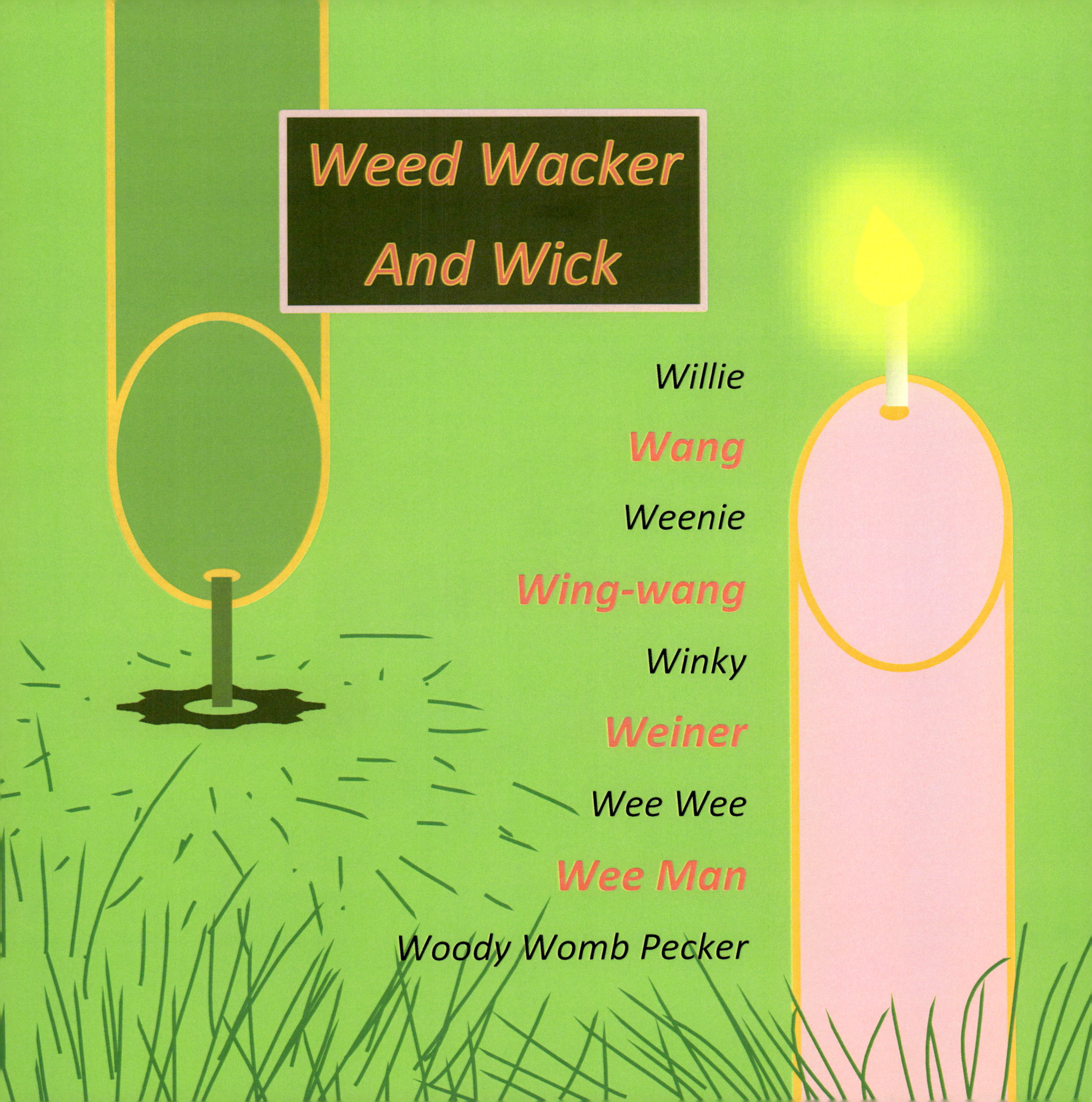

Weed Wacker
And Wick
Willie
Wang
Weenie
Wing-wang
Winky
Weiner
Wee Wee
Wee Man
Woody Womb Pecker

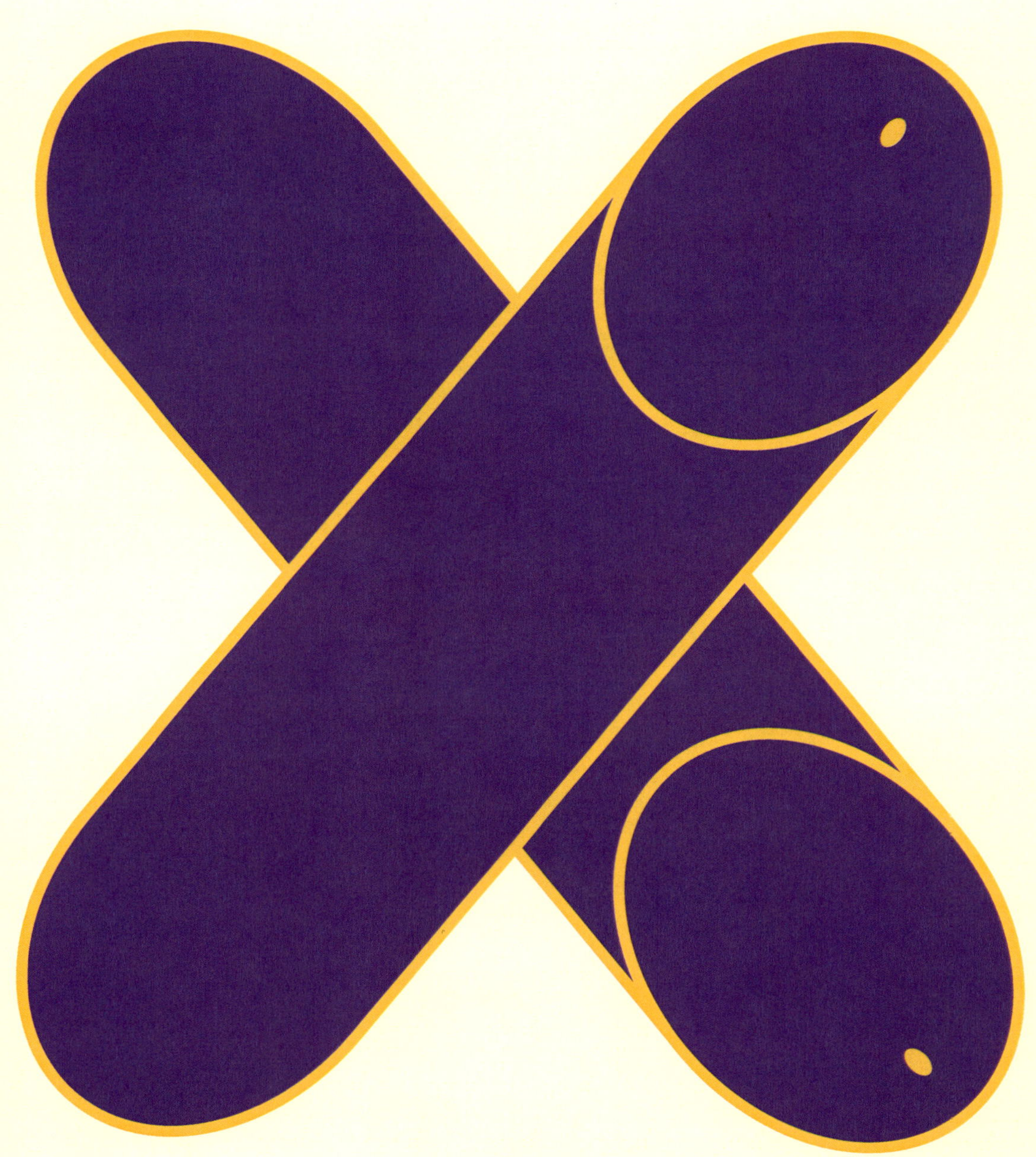

XYLOBHONE

Yogurt Launcher

Yardage

Yardstick

Yankster

Yo-Yo

Yeti

Yak

Zeus

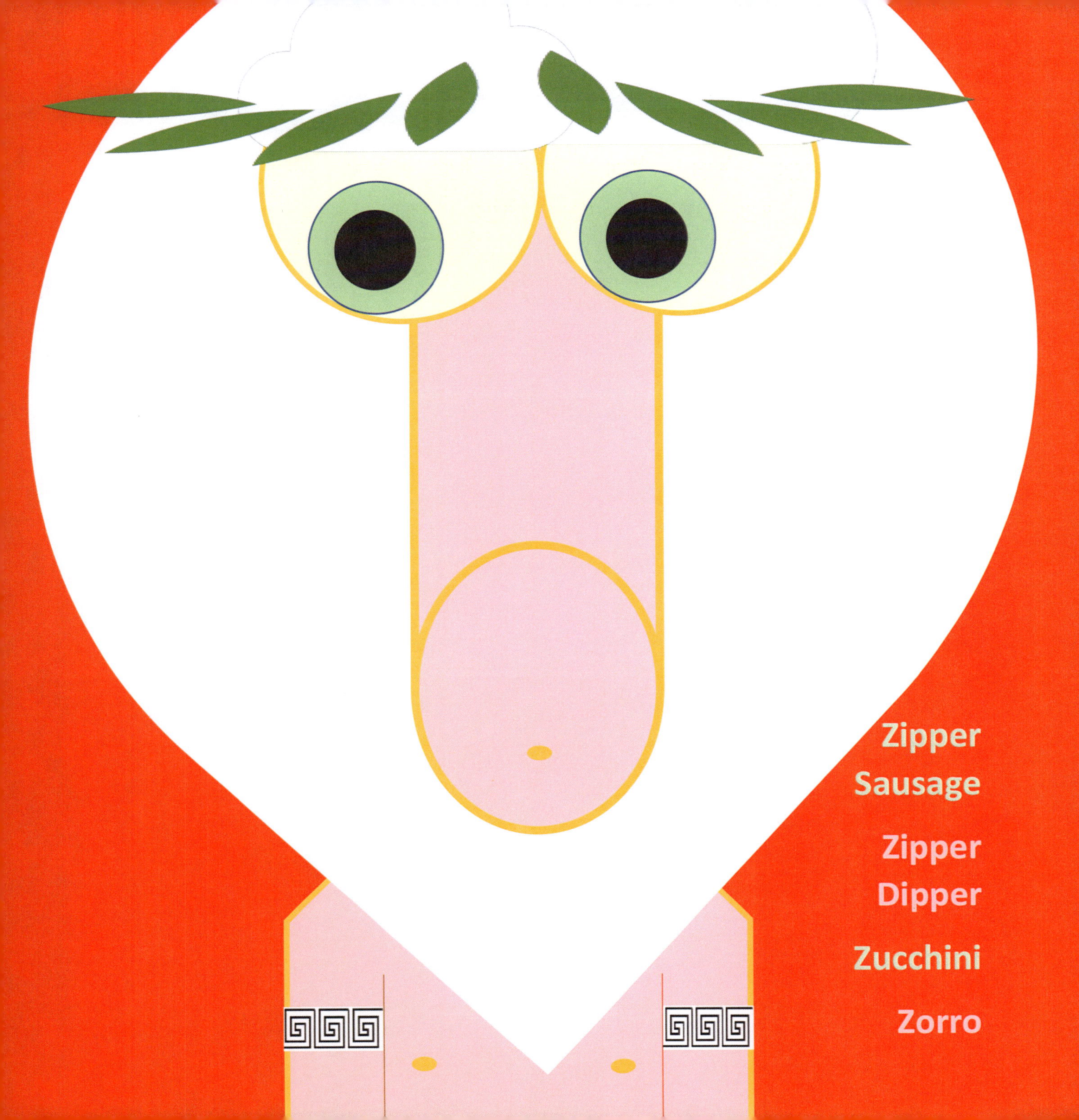

Zipper
Sausage

Zipper
Dipper

Zucchini

Zorro

Dick Literacy Categories

After researching and acquiring penis names, it became evident to me that the names could be shuffled into categories. In an attempt to do so, it was revealing that the creativity of the naming the penis came out of various motives, associations, feelings and fears. The following sampling of categories and their examples will reveal much about men as well as their creativity. Maybe you can expand the list.

Harold Cummings

Action – Slippapotamus, zipper dipper, juicer, custard launcher

Associative – Cigar, firehose, banana, cucumber, giraffe

Comedic – Woody Woodpecker, Hairy Canary

Conquest - Krull the Warrior King, killer, Master Blaster

Contentment - Joystick, boy toy, popsicle, best friend

Consistent Stamina - Faithful friend, iron fist, tin soldier

Contextual - King of the Jungle, knight, piston, Caligula

Cultural – Educated - Jack the Dripper (Jackson Pollock the Painter), Longfellow, matador, Zeus, Little Red Riding Hood

Destination – Uterus unicorn, anal impaler, pubic pony

Dreamer – The Big Dipper, redwood, yardstick, anaconda

Dirty - Gravy master, dirty dog, hog, tuna can, cum gun

Ejaculation - Mt. Etna, Mt. Erebus, custard launcher, sperminator, baster, Jack the Dripper, lube tube, Volcanic Nick

Erection - Stiffy, iron fist, hambone, erecto–magnificent

Enduring Significance – wood, Eifel's Tower, column, shaft

Friend - Fabulous Freddie, Frank, old fella

Humorous - Drippula, Harry Canary, pocket pony, sock puppet

Mechanical - Injector, rocket, crank, trouser train, vessel, drill

Mischievous – Knob goblin, weasel, crotch monkey, varmint

Nautical – Captain, craft, boat, stern, big dipper, whale, full sail

Neutral- Appendage, third leg, finger, vessel, junk, baby arm

Performance Acknowledgment – Quick dick, mini-me, unbelievable weevil, yankster, Old Faithful, Mr. Cumlately

Personality - Mr. Wonderful, ding-a-ling, happy, indulging devil

Prowess – Frequent flyer, filler thriller, cave dweller

Relationship - Mini-me, nutty buddy, best friend

Sexual Choice - Blow stick, anal impaler, but buddy, taco warmer

Size - Ankle spanker, anaconda, donkey dong, Long Dong Silver, peewee, straight eight, Girtha, Eiffel's Tower, zucchini

Visual - E.T., noodle, Snuffuleupagus, zucchini

Vaginal – Just-in-beaver, dipstick, babymaker, woody womb pecker, uterus unicorn

Value - Golden rod, stable cable

Whimsical – magical wand, unicorn, Captain Cucumber, silk whistle, lipstick, xylobhone

www.ingramcontent.com/pod-product-compliance
Lightning Source LLC
Chambersburg PA
CBRC090746110726
48005CB00008B/983